PIANO · VOCA

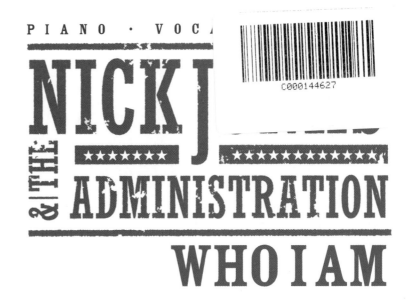

NICK J
& THE
ADMINISTRATION
WHO I AM

Photos by Olaf Henne, courtesy of Hollywood Records website.

ISBN 978-1-4234-9242-9

HAL•LEONARD®
CORPORATION

7777 W. BLUEMOUND RD. P.O. BOX 13819 MILWAUKEE, WI 53213

Visit Hal Leonard Online at
www.halleonard.com

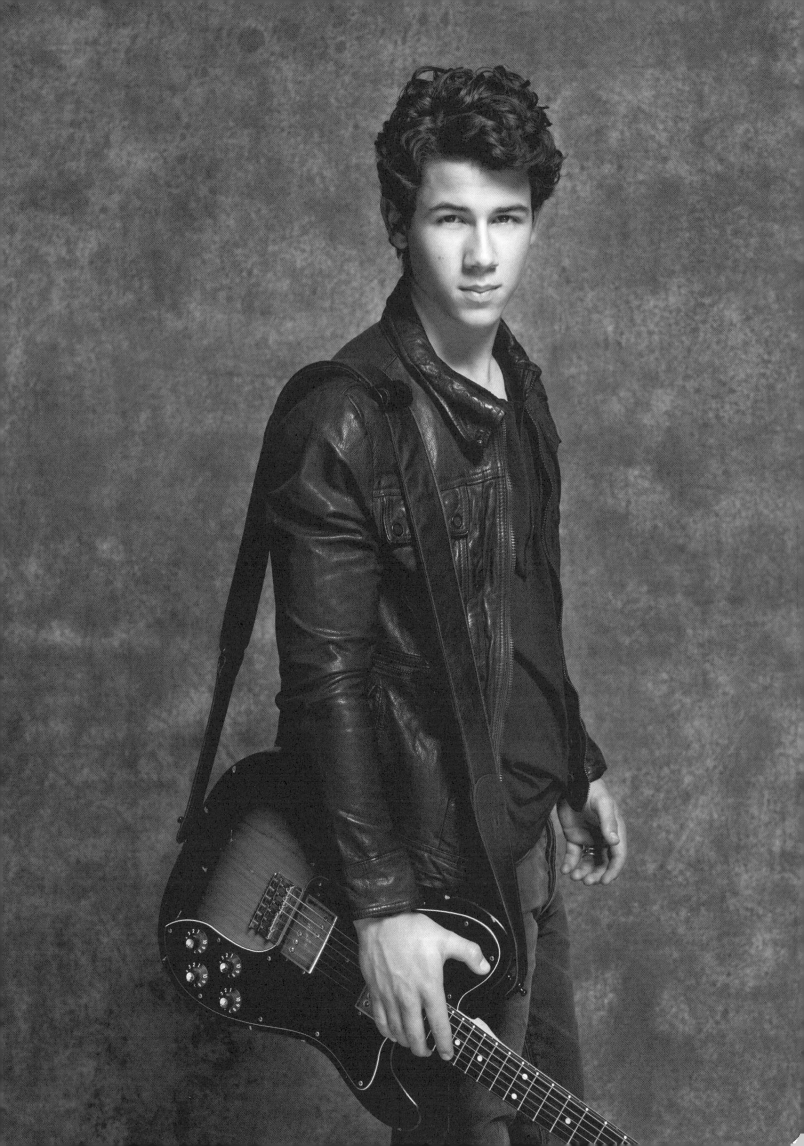

ROSE GARDEN

Words and Music by
NICHOLAS JONAS

WHO I AM

Words and Music by
NICHOLAS JONAS

Moderate groove

I want some-one __ to love __ me for who I am. __

I want some-one __ to need __ me.

Is that so bad? __ I wan-na break all __ the mad-

OLIVE AND AN ARROW

Words and Music by
NICHOLAS JONAS

Moderate Gospel feel

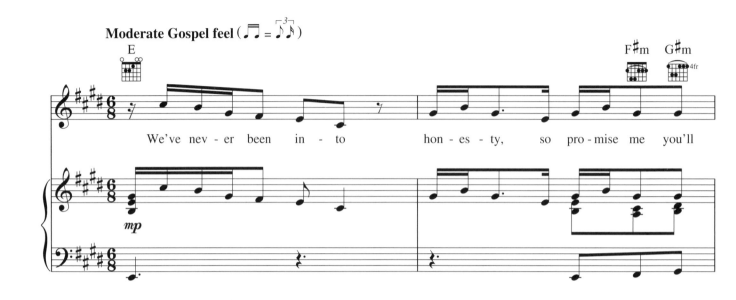

We've nev-er been in-to hon-es-ty, so pro-mise me you'll

let me know when you're ly - in'.

She wants to be an ea-gle and when she's high, she can fly no

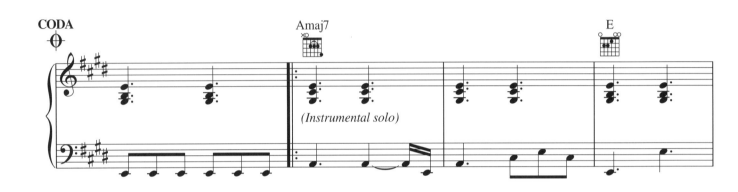

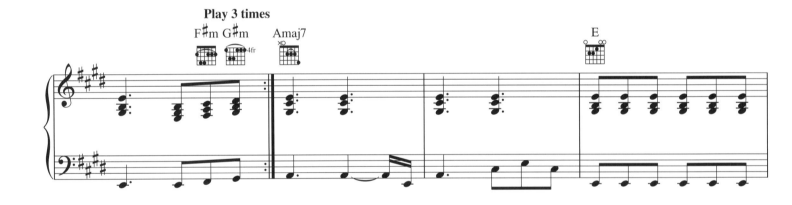

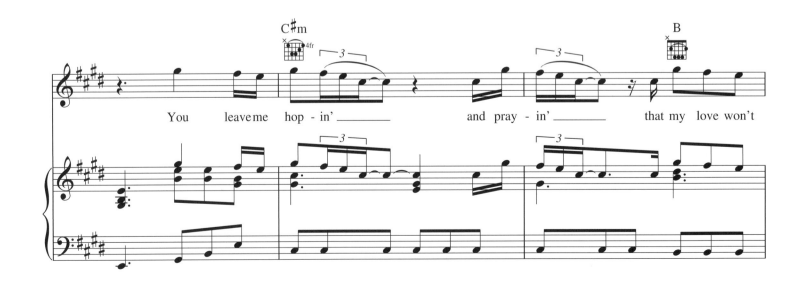

CONSPIRACY THEORY

Words and Music by
NICHOLAS JONAS

Driving Rock

IN THE END

Words and Music by NICHOLAS JONAS,
PJ BIANCO and GREG GARBOWSKY

LAST TIME AROUND

Words and Music by NICHOLAS JONAS,
PJ BIANCO and GREG GARBOWSKY

Some - how I missed it.
Can't you re - mem - ber?
Keep on mov - in' like you did last sum - mer when the

grass was green - er and your hair was long - er. If you be - come fa - mil - iar with an -

oth - er in town, ___ don't for - get a - bout the fun that we had ___ last time a - round. ___

(1st time only)

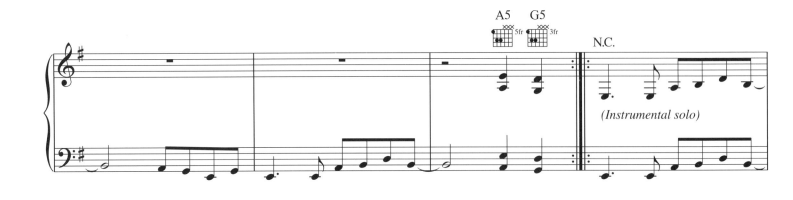

(Instrumental solo)

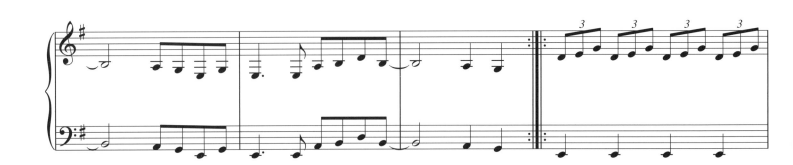

last time a - round.

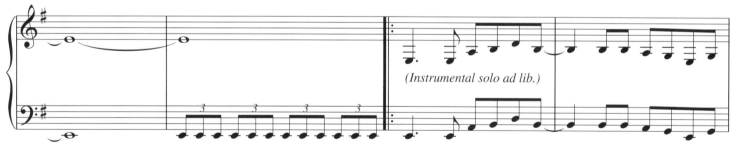

Last time a - round.

(Instrumental solo ad lib.)

Play 6 times

TONIGHT

Words and Music by NICHOLAS JONAS, JOSEPH JONAS,
KEVIN JONAS II and GREG GARBOWSKY

Well, here we are again
Ev-'ry sin-gle word's been said.

STATE OF EMERGENCY

Words and Music by NICHOLAS JONAS
and JOHN FIELDS

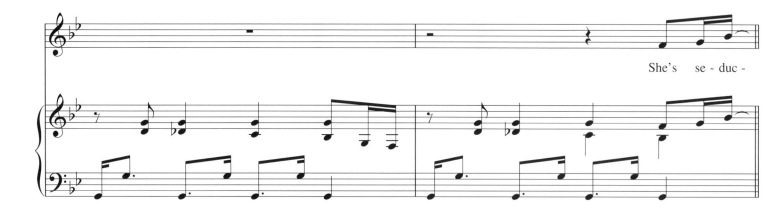

She's se - duc -

- tive;   she does it well.   She'll
her   but I'm still con - cerned   that
- ience   to the cause.   She'll

Recorded a half step higher.

VESPER'S GOODBYE

Words and Music by NICHOLAS JONAS
and PJ BIANCO

STRONGER
(Back on the Ground)

Words and Music by NICHOLAS JONAS,
JACK MOORING and LEELAND MOORING